John Sharp

A Sermon Preached Before the Right Honourable the Lord Mayor,

and Aldermen of London, at Bow Church.

John Sharp

A Sermon Preached Before the Right Honourable the Lord Mayor,
and Aldermen of London, at Bow Church.

ISBN/EAN: 9783337411411

Printed in Europe, USA, Canada, Australia, Japan

Cover: Foto ©Lupo / pixelio.de

More available books at **www.hansebooks.com**

A SERMON

Preached before the

RIGHT HONOURABLE

THE

Lord Mayor,

AND

ALDERMEN of LONDON,

AT

BOW-CHURCH.

By *JOHN SHARPE*, Chaplain to the
Right Honourable *Heneage* Lord *Finch*, Lord
High Chancellor of *ENGLAND*.

LONDON:
Printed by *Andrew Clark*, for *Walter Kettilby*, at
the Bishops Head in St. *Paul's* Church-Yard, 1676.

1 T I M. iv. 8.

Godlineſs is profitable unto all things, having a promiſe of the life that now is, and of that which is to come.

Heſe words are the enforcement of an exhortation which St. *Paul* had made to *Timothy* in the Verſe before going, which was that he ſhould *Avoid prophane and Old-wives Fables*; meaning thoſe Impious and ſuperſtitious *Doctrines*, and the carnal and unchriſtian *Obſervances* that were grounded upon them (ſome of which he had mentioned in the beginning of this Chapter) which ſome at that time did endeavour to introduce into *Chriſtianity*: and inſtead of applying his mind to theſe, that he ſhould rather *Exerciſe himſelf unto* true *Godlineſs*.

This was the Exhortation. The Arguments wherewith he enforceth it are Two : Firſt, The Unprofitableneſs of theſe Carnal and Superſti-

tious

rious *Doctrines* and *Practices*. *Bodily exercise* (faith he) *profiteth little*. Secondly, The real usefulness of solid Vertue and Godlines to all the Purposes of life. *Godlines is profitable to all things, having a promise of this Life as well as of that which is to come*.

I shall not here meddle at all with the former part of the Apostles *Exhortation* or the *Argument* that hath relation to it ; but shall apply my self wholly to the latter, craving leave most plainly and affectionately to press upon you the *Exercise* of *Godlines* upon those Grounds and Considerations on which the Apostle here recommendeth it.

Indeed to a man that considers well, it will appear the most unaccountable thing in the world,that among all those several *Exercises* that Mankind busie themselves about,this of *Godlines* should be in so great a measure neglected, that men should be so diligent, so industrious, so unwearied, some in getting *Estates*, others in Purveying for *Pleasures*, others in learning *Arts* and *Trades* ; All in some thing or other relating to this *sensible* World ; and so few should study to acquaint themselves with *God*,and the Concernments of their souls, to learn the *Arts* of Virtue and Religious Conversation.

Cer-

Certain it is, this *Piece* of *Skill* is not more above our reach than many of thofe other things we fo induftrioufly purfue;nay,I am apt to think it is more within our power than moft of them. For in our other Labours we cannot always promife to our felves certain fuccefs. A thou-fand things may intervene which we know not of, that may defeat all our plots and defigns though never fo carefully laid; but no man ever . ferioufly undertook the Bufinefs of Religion but he accomplifhed it.

Nay further, As we can with greater certain-ty, fo can we with lefs pains and difficulty pro-mife to our felves fuccefs in this affair, than we can hope to compafs moft of our worldly de-figns which fo much take up our thoughts. I doubt not in the leaft but that lefs labour, lefs trouble, lefs folicitude will ferve to make a man a good *Chriftian*, than to get an *Eftate*, or to attain a competent skill in Humane Arts and Sciences.

And then for other Motives to oblige us to the ftudy of *Religion*, we have incomparably more and greater than we can have for the pur-fuit of any other thing. It is certainly the grea-teft Concernment we have in the world. It is the very thing God fent us into the world about. It is the very thing that his Son came down

for

from Heaven to inftruct us, in. It is the very
thing by which we fhall be concluded everlaftingly happy, or everlaftingly miferable after
this life is ended.

These things well confidered, we may juftly
(I fay) ftand amazed, that men fhould be fo
prodigioufly fupine and negligent in an Affair
of this nature and importance, as we fee they
generally are.

If there can any account be given of this
matter, I fuppofe it muft be fome fuch as this,
That the *things* of this *World,* upon which we be-
ftow our Care, our Time, our Courtfhip, are
prefent to us. We fee them every day before
our eyes; we tafte, we feel the fweetnefs of
them; we are fenfible that their enjoyment is
abfolutely neceffary to our prefent well-being:
But as for fpiritual matters they lie under a great
difadvantage. They appear to us as at a great
diftance. We do not apprehend any prefent
need we have of them : Nor do we fancy any
fweetnefs or relifh in them. Nay, on the contrary, we form the moft frightful and difmal
Images of them that can be. We look upon them
not only as *flat,* and *unfavoury*; but as things
which if we trouble our heads too much about
will certainly ruine all our defigns in this
World.

World. We think *Religion* good for nothing but
to spoil good Company ; to make us melancholy and mopish ; to distract us in our Busi-
nefs and Employments ; and to put fo many
Reftraints upon us that we can neither with
that freedom nor fuccefs purfue our Temporal
Concernments, which we think neceffary to our
happinefs in this World.

But let us suppofe things to be thus with Religion as we have fancied, yet cannot this be
any reafonable Excufe for our carelefnefs about
it. What though there were no vifible Benefit
by a religious life in this world ? What though
the rewards of our pains about it were only in
reverfion ? Yet fince a time will come when
it will be our greateft Intereft to have been
heartily Religious, is it not a madnefs now to
neglect it ? What though *Religion* be a courfe of
life difficult and unpleafant ; a way ftrewed
with Briers and Thorns ; a way which if we
follow, we are certainly loft, as to our hopes of
any thing here ? Yet fince a Time will certainly come when we fhall wifh, that we had been
good *Chriftians*, though we had loft our *right eyes*
and our *right hands* upon the condition ; when
we fhall wifh that we had purchafed Virtue
though at the rate of the lofs of the whole
World.

World : For Gods fake why fhould we not be
of the fame mind now ? Who but Fools and
Children but will look upon that which fhall
certainly and unavoidably be, with the fame
regard as if it was now prefent ?

But indeed, this is not the Cafe of Religion;
This Bufinefs of Piety is not fo formidable as
we often reprefent it. It is no fuch Enemy to
our Temporal defigns. It is a very innocent
thing, and will do us no harm; though we
look no further than this prefent World. It will
hinder none of our delights or pleafures, but
will allow us to gratifie every *Appetite* that God
and Nature hath put into us. And if any man
doubt this, let him name that Natural defire,
which the Chriftian Religion doth forbid or any
way hinder the innocent fatisfaction of : I am
confident he fhall be able to name none. Since
this is the Cafe then, how much more *Childifh*
than *Children* fhall we appear if we make fo
little reckoning of it ? How inexcufably Foolifh fhall we be, if we will not be at fome pains
to poffefs our felves of that which will be no
manner of Hinderance to us in our affairs in this
World, and will infallibly make us everlaftingly
happy in that which is to come ?

But

But further ; What if it be certain, that a Life of ſtrict virtue is not only no Hinderance to our Temporal deſigns, but a great furtherance of them? What if it can be Proved, that beſides the influence it has on our Happineſs in the next Life, it is alſo the beſt thing in the World to ſerve our turns in this? And that nothing can ſo much contribute to the bringing about our *Worldly Aims* ; no ſuch ready way to attain to what our very *Fleſh* and *Bloud* moſt deſires, moſt delights in, as to be ſincerely *Pious.* What imaginable pretence can we then have for our contempt of *God* and *Virtue* ? If this can be made to appear, ſure all our Objections will be fully anſwered ; all our ſcruples ſatisfied ; all our prejudices againſt *Religion* wholly removed ; and every one that is not abandoned of his *Fortune* and his *Senſes,* as well as his *Reaſon,* muſt think himſelf concerned to become a Votary to it ; ſince he can have no Temptation or Motive to *Vice* which will not more powerfully draw him to *Virtue* ; and all the *ends* that the *one* can pretend to *ſerve,* will much more effectually be *ſerved* by the *other* ; and he eſcapes an Eternity of Miſery, and gets everlaſting Life into the Bargain.

I think.

I think it therefore worth the while to spend the time now allotted me in making good this Point, and discovering something at least of that universal *Profitableness of* ˈ*Godliness* to the purposes of *Human Life*, that St. *Paul* in my Text assures us of.

But because the *Studies* of men are so infinitely various, and the *Ends* of *Life* to be served so many, that it will be impossible to speak *particularly* of them; it will be needful to pitch upon some *general* Heads, such as, if they do not comprehend *all*, may yet take in *most* of those things, to which the Labours and Endeavours of men are directed, and in the acquisition of which they have compassed their Designs; and to shew the *serviceableness* of *Religion* above all other means for the attaining of them. And I think, I cannot pitch better than upon those three noted *Idols* of the World, *Wealth* and *Honour* and *Pleasure*; these being the *Goods* which have always been accounted to divide Mankind among them; and into the service of some one or *all* of which All that set up for a happy life in this world do list themselves, how different and disagreeing soever they be from one another as to their particular Employments and ways of Living. I shall therefore make it

appear,

appear, that *Godliness* and *Religion* is a very great furtherance to the acquisition of all these; and that no man can take a more ready way either to *improve* his *Fortune*, or to *purchase* a *Name and Reputation among men*, or to *live comfortably* and *pleasantly* in this world, than heartily to serve *God*, and to live in the practice of every Virtue.

And in the *First* place, I begin with the *Conducivenefs of Religion and Godlinefs to improve our outward Fortunes*; the Advantages of it for the *getting* or *encreasing* an *Estate* : For this is the thing to which our Thoughts are commonly first directed, as looking upon it as the Foundation of a happy Life in this world.

But here I desire not to be mistaken : I would not be thought to deal with you as one of our ordinary *Empiricks*, that promises many brave feats in his *Bill*, which are indeed beyond the power of his *Art:* I do not pretend that *Wealth* and *Opulency* is necessarily entailed upon *Religion;* so that whoever is *good* shall presently be inabled to make Purchases, and to leave Lands and Livings to his Children. *Riches* are one of those things that are not so perfectly in our power, that all men may hope for an equal share

of

of them. The having more or lefs depends of-
tentimes not fo much upon our felves, as upon
that condition and quality in which we were
born, the way and courfe of Life into which
our Friends put us; and a hundred accidental
circumftances to which we our felves contribute
nothing. But this I fay; fuppofing the vertuous man in equal circumftances with others;
fuppofing him to ftand upon the fame level, and
to enjoy the fame fortuitous hits and external
concurrences that they do, and he fhall by many odds have the advantage of them for thriving
and improving in the world in any condition of
life whatfoever.

So that, fo far as the getting of Riches depends upon Humane endeavours; fo far as it is
an *Art*, and falls under *Precepts* and *Directions*:
no man alive can propofe a better expedient in
order thereto than a ferious practife of Religion.

To make this good, let it be confidered, that
as to the *means* that do in a more direct and im-
mediate manner influence upon the getting or
improving an Eftate (I fpeak of *General means*,
fuch as are of ufe in all conditions of life; for to
meddle with the Myfteries of any Particular
Art or Trade, is not my purpofe, as indeed it
is beyond my skill :) as to fuch means as thefe, I
fay

say, none can prescribe more effectual than these four.

1. *Prudence*, in administring our Affairs.
2. *Diligence*, in that Vocation wherein God hath placed us.
3. *Thrift* and good *Husbandry*.
4. Keeping a good Correspondence with those in whose power it is to hinder or promote our Affairs.

If now it do appear that *Godliness* doth highly improve a man in all these four respects; if it can be shewed that all these *Fruits* naturally grow and thrive better in a *Religious* Soil then any other, it will evidently follow; that supposing these above-named means do indeed contribute to the making of a Fortune, (and if they do not, no man knows what doth; and we strangely abuse our Friends and our Children, when upon that account we recommend them to them) it follows, I say, that a life of Godliness is a mighty advantage to a man for the purposes I am speaking of.

And first of all, it will be easie to shew that *Godliness* doth above all things tend to *make a man wise and prudent, skilful and dexterous in the management of his Affairs of what nature soever:*

for

for it doth very much clear and improve a mans
underſtanding, not only by a certain natural ef-
ficacy it hath (as I ſhall ſhew hereafter) to puri-
fie the *Blood* and *Spirits*, upon which the perfecti-
on of our Intellectual Operations doth exceedingly much depend ; but alſo by diſpelling thoſe
adventitious clouds that ariſe in the diſcerning fa-
culty from the noiſome *Fumes* of Luſt and Paſſion.

All Vice in the very nature of it, depraves and
diſtorts a mans judgment, fills our minds with
prejudices, and falſe Apprehenſions of things ;
and, no man that is under the dominion of it,
can poſſibly have ſuch a free uſe of his Reaſon
as otherwiſe he might; for he will commonly
ſee things, not as they are in themſelves, but
in thoſe diſguiſes and falſe colours which his
Paſſion puts upon them : Upon which account
he cannot avoid but he will be often impoſed
upon, and commit a thouſand errors in the management of his Affairs, which the vertuous
man, whoſe Reaſon is pure and untinctur'd, is
ſecured from. It cannot be imagined that either he ſhould foreſee events ſo clearly, or ſpy
opportunities ſo ſagaciouſly, or weigh things ſo
impartially, or deliberate ſo calmly, or tranſ-
act ſo cautiouſly, as the man that is free from
thoſe

thofe manifold prepoffeffions which his mind is fraught with.

We fee this every day verified in men of all Ranks and Conditions, of all Callings and Employments. What a multitude of inconveniences, as to matter of dealing between man and man, doth an intemperate Appetite betray men to? How filly and foolifh is the moft fhrewd man, when Wine hath gotten into his head? There is none fo fimple in his company, but fuppofing him to be fober, and to have defigns upon him, he fhall be able to over-reach him. What a world of Advantages doth the Angry man give to him he deals with, by the haftinefs and impatience of his fpirit? How often doth a man do that in the fury and expectancies of a Luft, for which when his Ardors are over, he is ready to bite his nails for very vexation?

It is thus more or lefs with all kind of Vices, they craze a mans head, and caft a mift before his eyes, and make him often lofe himfelf in thofe very ways wherein he pretends to be moft skilful: So that it cannot be denied, that vertue is of a fingular ufe in all matters wherein we have occafion to make ufe of our Reafon, and doth fecure us from a multitude of indifcretions, which without it we fhould unavoidably commit.

C 3 But

(14)

But secondly, *Godliness is also an excellent means to secure a mans diligence in the discharge of his Calling and Employment*, which is also a matter of very great confequence in order to our thriving in the world : for it is the *diligent hand that maketh rich*, and the *man that is diligent in his bufinefs, that fhall ftand before Kings*; as *Solomon* tells us.

Now the Obligations that *Religion* layeth upon us to be careful in this point, are far ftronger then what can arife from any other refpect or confideration foever ; for it obligeth us to mind our Bufinefs, not only for our *own* but for *Gods* fake : it chargeth the matter upon our Confciences, and reprefents it to us as a part of that fervice we owe to our *Creator* ; and upon the due performance of which, no lefs then the everlafting welfare of our fouls doth depend : for it affures us, that he that will call us to account for every *idle Word*, will much more do fo for the *idle* expence of our *Time*, and the abufe or not improvement of thofe Talents that he hath entrufted us with. So that though we had no worldly inducement to make us diligent in our *Callings*, though we were fure we fhould fuffer no prejudice in our Temporal Affairs by *Idlenefs*, and the neglect of our Bufinefs, (the fear of which yet is the only principle that puts

world-

worldly men upon action) nevertheless we
were infinitely concerned not to be flack or negligent in this matter, in regard it is a point that
will be so severely exacted of us in the other
world.

I know but one Objection that can be made
against this discourse, and it is this, that what
engagements soever *Religion* lays upon us to the
careful spending of our time, yet its own *Exercises, Prayer.* and *Reading*, and *Meditation*, take
up so great a portion of it, which might be spent
in the works of our ordinary Employment,
that in effect it rather hinders our attendance on
our Business than promotes it. But to this it is
easily answered, that there is no man so enga-
ged in the world, but may if he please, make
both his *Business* and his *Devotions* consist toge-
ther without prejudicing of either.

They have very false Apprehensions of Religion, that think it obliges us to be always upon
our knees, or always poring upon some good
Book : no, we do as truly serve God, and per-
form acts of Religion, when we labour honestly
in our Vocation, as when we go to Church, or
say our Prayers.

It is true indeed, we ought to have our hearts
in Heaven as much as is possible, and to that end
we

we ought to pray continually; but what hinders but we may do this in the midst of our Busines? There is no employment doth so entire-
ly engross a mans mind, but he may find leisure
if he please, many times a day, to entertain
good thoughts, to quicken and reinforce his purposes, to cast up a short Prayer or a wish to
God Almighty. And this I dare say for your
encouragement, that such a devout frame of
heart, such frequent and sudden dartings of
your souls to God, while you are at your Business, will be so far from hindering or distract-
ing you in it, that they will make you go about
it with much more vigour and alacrity.

But further, I would ask any man that makes
the foresaid Objection, supposing *Religion* ten
times more expensive of our time then really it
is, yet whether *Vice* and *Sin* be not much more
so, then it would be. What a multitude of idle
avocations from, and interruptions in our Busines doth that daily occasion unto men? what
a number of impertinent Discourses, unprofit-
able Visits, needless points of Gallantry, long
diversions by Drink, and Play, and Company;
not to mention a great many other Debauches,
doth it frequently engage men in? and yet these
we count no hinderances to our Busines; these
we

we complain not of; but to spend a quarter of that time in some devout Exercise, this is intolerable, it wasts too much of our time, our occasions will not permit it. Such partial and unjust estimators of things are we. But I proceed:

In the third place then, as for *Frugality* and *good Husbandry*, which is another necessary requisite for the getting of *Wealth*. *Religion* is unquestionably the belt mistress of it in the world; for it retrencheth all the exorbitances and wantonnesses of our Desires, which are the things that pick the money out of our purses, and teacheth us to live after the measures of *Nature*, which every body knows are little, and cheap. It perfectly cuts off all those idle expences with which the Estates of other men stand almost continually charged. The *Modesty* of it cloaths us at a small rate; and its *Temperance* spreads for us, though a neat, yet a frugal Table. The attendance it requires on our Business will not allow us to embezel our money in Drinking or Gaming: nor will that *Purity* which is inseparable from it ever let us know what the vast and sinking expences of lewdness and uncleanness are. In a word, it is *Vice* only that is the chargeable thing; it is only *Shame* and *Repentance* that

D   men

men buy at fuch coftly rates. Godlinefs is fa-
ving, and full of good Husbandry; nor has it
any known or unknown ways of fpending, ex-
cept it be thofe of *Charity*, which indeed, in
proper fpeaking, are not fo much expence, as
Ufury; for money fo laid out, doth always even
in this life return to us with Advantage.

The fourth and laft means I mentioned of
Thriving in the world, was the *keeping a good
Correfpondence with all thofe in whofe power it is to
hinder or promote our Affairs.* This every body
knows to be a prime point in *Policy*; and indeed
it is of a large extent, and of continual ufe. No
man can be fuppofed fo independent on others,
but that as he is fome way beholden to them
for all that he has, fo he ftands in need of their
help and concurrence for all that he hopes for.
Men do not make their fortunes of themfelves,
nor grow rich by having Treafures dropped in
their Laps, but they do it by the benefit of Humane Society, by the mutual affiftances and
good offices that one man performs for another.
So that whoever intends to thrive in the world,
it above all things imports him fo to carry himfelf towards all that he hath any commerce
with, fo far to fecure their favour and good will
that

that they may be obliged not to deny him any
of thofe affiftances, which the exigency of his
Affairs calls for at their hands. But now how
this fhould be done any otherwife than by being
truly *Juft* and *Honeft*, by abftaining from *Violence* and *Injury*, by being *True* to our *Trufts*, and
Faithful in performing our *Contracts*; and in a
word, by doing all thofe good *Offices* to others
which we expect they fhould do unto us, which
as our Saviour tells us is the fum of *Religion*, is
a very hard thing to conceive.

The ufefulnefs or rather the neceffity of fuch
a Behaviour as this, in order to the gaining the
good *Opinion* of others, and fo ferving our own
ends by them, is fo univerfally acknowledged,
that even thofe that make no real Confcience
of thefe things, are yet neverthelefs in all their
dealings forced to pretend to them. *Open* and
Bare-fac'd Knavery rarely ferves a mans turn in
this world, but it is under the mask of *Virtue*
and *Honefty* that it ufually performs thofe Feats
it doth; which is no lefs than a Demonftration
of the conducivenefs of thofe things to promote
our Temporal Interefts : for if the meer *Pretence* to them be a great advantage to us for this
purpofe, it cannot be imagined but that the
Reality of them will be a greater. Certainly

D 2   the

(·20·)

the *Power* of *Godliness* will be able to do more than the *Form* alone, and that if it was upon no other account than this, that no man that is but a meer *Pretender* to *Honesty* can long hope to keep his credit among men. It is impossible to *act* a *Part* for any long time; let him carry it never so cunningly, his *Vizor* will some time or other be thrown off, and he will appear in his true colours; and to what a world of mischiefs and inconveniences he will then be exposed, every one that knows how hated, how detested, how abandon'd by every one, a *Knave* and a *Villain* is, may easily determine. I hope I need say no more to convince you that *Religion* is the best *Policy*, and that the more hearty and confciencious any man is in the practice of it, the more likely he is to *Thrive* and *Improve* in the world.

So that I may now proceed to the *second* general point to be spoken to, which is the *Profitableness of Religion for the attaining a good Name and Reputation*. How very much it conduceth to this purpose will appear from these two considerations.

First, it lays the *surest Grounds* and *Foundations* for a *good Name* and *Reputation*.

Second-

Secondly, Men are generally so just to it, that it rarely misses of a good Name and Reputation. The first is an argument from *Reason*, the second from *Experience*.

First of all *Godliness* layeth the *truest Foundations* for a *fair Reputation* in the world. There are but two things that can give a man a title to the good *Opinion* and *Respects* of men; the inward *Worth* and *Dignity* of his *Person*, and his *Usefulness* and *Serviceableness* to others. The first of these challengeth mens *Esteem*, the other their *Love*. Now both these Qualities Religion and Virtue do eminently possess us of.

For first, the *Religious* man is certainly the most *Worthy* and *Excellent* Person; for he of all others lives most up to the great *End* for which he was designed, which is the natural measure of the *Goodness* and *Worth* of Things.

What ever external Advantages a man may have, yet if he be not endowed with virtuous Qualities, he is far from having any True Worth or Excellence, and consequently cannot be a fit object of our *Praise* and *Esteem*; because he wants that which should make him *Perfect* and *Good* in his *Kind*. For it is not a comely Personage, or a long Race of Famous Ancestors, or a large Revenue, or a multitude

of

of Servants, or many swelling Titles, or any other thing without a man that speaks him a *Compleat Man*, or makes him to *be* what he should be; but the right use of his Reason, the employing his Liberty and Choice to the best purposes, the Exercising his Powers and Faculties about the *fittest Objects*, and in the most *due measures*. These are the Things that make him *Excellent*. Now none can be said to do this but only he that is Virtuous.

Secondly, Religion also is that which makes a man most *Useful* and *Profitable* to others; for it effectually secures his performance of all those Duties whereby both the security and welfare of the *Publick*, and also the Good and Advantage of *particular* Persons is most attained.

It makes men Lovers of their Country, Loyal to their Prince, Obedient to Laws; it is the surest Bond and Preservative of Society in the world; it obliges us to live peaceably, and to submit our selves to our Rulers, not only for *wrath*, but also for *Conscience* sake: It renders us modest and governable in Prosperity, and resolute and couragious to suffer bravely in a good cause in the worst of times: It teacheth us to endeavour as much as in us lies to promote

the

the good of every particular Member of the
Community, to be inflexibly upright, to do
hurt to none, but good offices to all, to be cha-
ritable to the Bodies and Souls of men, to do
all manner of kindneffes that lie within our
power: it takes off the fowrnefs and morofenefs of our Spirits, and makes us Affable and
Courteous, Gentle and Obliging, and willing
to embrace with open Arms and an hearty Love,
all forts and conditions of men.

In every Relation wherein we can ftand to
one another, it influenceth upon us in order to
the making us more ufeful; it makes *Parents*
kind, and Indulgent, and careful of the Educa-
tion of their *Children*, and Children Loving and
Obedient to their *Parents* : it makes Servants
diligent to *pleafe their Mafters, and to do their work
in finglenefs of heart, not with eye-fervice as men-plea-
fers, but as unto God*; and it makes Mafters gentle and forbearing, and careful to make provi-
fion for their Family, *as thofe that know they have
a Mafter in Heaven, that is no refpecter of perfons.*
In a word, there is no condition or capacity, in
which Religion will not be fignally an inftru-
ment of making us more ferviceable to others,
and of doing more good in the world. And if
fuch be the fpirit and temper of it, how is it
pof-

possible but it must needs acquire a great deal of Respect and Love from all forts of men ? If Obligingnefs and doing good in ones Generation do not endear a man to thofe that know him; do not entitle him to their Love and Affections, what thing in the world is there that is likely to do it ?

But secondly, *True and unaffected Goodnefs feldom miffes of a good Reputation in the world.* How unjuft to Virtue foever men are in other refpects, yet in this they generally give it its due; where ever it appears it generally meets with Efteem and Approbation ; nay it has the good word of many that otherwife are not over-fond of Religion. Though they have not the grace to be *Good* themfelves, yet they rarely have the confidence not to commend *Goodnefs* in others.

Add to this, that no man ever raifed to himfelf a *Good name* in the world, but it was upon the fcore of his *Virtues*, either *Real* or *Pretended*. Vice hath fometimes got *Riches*, and advanced it felf into *Preferments*, but it never was accounted *Honourable* in any Nation.

It muft be acknowledged indeed that it may and doth fometimes happen, that *Vicious* men may be had in *Efteem*; but then it is to be confidered,

fidered, that it is not for their *Vices* that they
are efteemed , but for fome *good Quality* or
other they are eminent in. And there is no
doubt , if thofe men were without thofe *Vices*,
their *Reputation* would be fo far from being
thereby *diminifhed*, that it would become much
more *Confiderable*.

It muft alfo be acknowledged on the other
hand , that even *Virtuous* and *Good* men may
fometimes fail of that *Efteem* and *Refpect* that
their Virtue feems to merit , nay, in that degree
as to be flighted and defpifed, and to have many
Odious Terms and *Nick-names* put upon them :
But when we confider the cafes in which this
happens, it will appear to be of no force at all
for the difproving what has been now deliver-
ed. For *firft* , it ought to be confidered what
kind of *Perfons* thofe are that treat *Virtue* and *Vir-*
tuous men thus *Contemptuoufly* , we fhall always
find them to be the *Worft* and the *Vileft* of mankind ; fuch who have debauched the natural
principles of their minds , have loft all the no-
tions and diftinctions of *Good* and *Evil*, are fal-
len below the *Dignity* of *Humane Nature*, and
have nothing to bear up themfelves with , but
Boldnefs and *Confidence* , *Drollery* and *Scurrility*,
and turning into *Ridicule* every thing that is

E   grave

grave and serious : But it is with thefe as it is
with the *Monfters* and *Extravagances* of *Nature*,
they are but very *Few*. Few in comparifon of
the reft of mankind, who have wifer and truer
fentiments of things. But if they were more
numerous, no man of underftanding would va-
lue what fuch men faid of him. It looks like
a Crime to be commended by *fuch* Perfons, and
may juftly occafion a man to reflect upon his
own actions, and to cry out to himfelf as *He*
did of old, What have I done that thefe men
fpeak well of me ?

But fecondly, it cannot be denied but that
fome perfons who are otherwife *Virtuous* and
Religious, may be guilty of fuch Indifcretions as
thereby to give others occafion to *flight* and *de-
fpife* them. But then it is to be confidered, that
this is not to be charged upon *Virtue* and *Religion*, but is the *Particular Fault* of the *Perfons*.
Every one that is *Religious* is not *Prudent*; the
meannefs of a mans *Underftanding*, or his Rafh
and Intemperate *Zeal*, or the morofenefs of his
Temper, or his too great *Scrupulofity* about little
things, may fometimes make his Behaviour
Uncouth and *Fantaftick*, and betray him to do
many actions which he may think his *Religion*
obliges him to, that other People will be apt
to.

to fancy *Silly* and *Ridiculous*. But this doth not at all reflect upon *Religion* ; nor doth it follow, that because the *Imprudence* of this or the other Particular man , expofes him to the *Mirth* and the *Pleafantnefs* of others, that therefore all *Religious Perfons* muſt fall under the fame *Fate*. Moſt certainly *Religion*, wherever it is governed by *Knowledge* and *found Principles*, wherever it is managed with *Prudence* and *Difcretion* , is a thing fo *Noble*, fo *Amiable*, that it attracts *Love*, and commands *Refpect* from all that are acquainted with it , unlefs they be ſuch profligately wicked Perfons as I juſt now fpoke of.

There is one *Objection* made from the *Scripture* againſt this and the former *Point* I have been fpeaking to, which I defire to remove, before I proceed to the *third* General Head of my Diſcourfe. It is this : That the Scripture is fo far from reprefenting *Godlinefs* as a means to *Improve our Fortunes*, or *attain a Reputation in the world*, that it feems directly to affirm the contrary; for it affures us, that *All thofe that will live godly in Chriſt muſt fuffer Perfecution*. *That the Difciples of Chriſt ſhall be Hated of All men for His Names fake*. That *the World ſhall revile and perfecute them , and fpeak all manner of Evil of them*; and that *through*

many

many Tribulations we must enter into the Kingdom *of* God.

But to this it is easily answered, that these and other such like Passages of *Scripture* do not speak the *General* and *Common* Fate that attends Godliness in all *times* and *places* of the world, according to the *Ordinary* course of Gods Providence ; but only refer to that *particular Time,* when *Christianity* was to be planted in the world ; then, indeed, *Persecution* and *Disgrace*, loss of *Goods,* and even of *Life* it self, was to be the common portion of those that professed it : nor could it otherwise be expected ; for, when a new *Religion* is to be set up, and such a Religion as is perfectly *destructive* of all those others that have been by long *custom* received, and are by *Laws* established in the world, It cannot be imagined but that it will meet with a great deal of Contradiction and Opposition from all sorts of persons. But this was a peculiar and extraordinary case, and could but last for a certain time ; now that Christianity hath obtained in the world, and is adopted into the Laws of Kingdoms, as God be thanked it is among us at this day : so far need we be from fearing that the practice of it will draw upon us any *Persecution,* or such other Inconveniences as are mentioned

tioned in the fore-cited places, that there is no doubt but that we may Rationally expect from it all those *External* Benefits and Advantages, which as we have seen it is in its own nature apt to produce, and which God hath indeed made over to it by *Promise*, in several Paſſages of the Scripture, eſpecially of the Old Teſtament.

For that I may mention this by the By, I do not conceive that thoſe Promiſes of *Long Life, Good Days*, and all manner of worldly *Proſperity*, with which the Practice of *Godlineſs* is ſo frequently enforced in the *Old Teſtament*, were ſo appropriated to the *Jewiſh* Religion, as to be antiquated or diſannulled by the Introduction of the *Chriſtian*; but rather that they are ſtill in force to all the Purpoſes they were then : For that the coming of *Chriſt* into the world did add many great *Bleſſings* and *Priviledges* to the People of God, which before they had not, we are certain of : but that it *took away* from them any that before they had, this we no where read, nor indeed is it probable.

But I haſten to the third and laſt General Head I am to ſpeak to, which is the *Excellent Miniſteries of Religion above all other things, to the Pleaſures of Humane Life* : which point, if it be

clearly

clearly made out, I do not see what can be further wanting to recommend it unto us, as the most effectual Instrument for the serving all our turns in this World. Now that Godliness doth indeed make the most excellent Provisions for all sorts of Pleasures, will appear by these four Considerations.

First, That it eminently ministreth to *Health*, which is a necessary Foundation for all *Pleasures*.

Secondly, It doth much increase the *Relish* and *Sweetness* of all our other *Pleasures*.

Thirdly, It secures us from all those *Inquietudes* and *Disturbances* which are apt to *embitter* our *Pleasures*, and make our Lives uncomfortable.

Fourthly, It adds to *Humane Life* a world of *Pleasures* of its own, which those that are not possessed of it, are utterly unacquainted with.

First of all, *Godliness doth very much conduce to Health*, which is so necessary to our enjoyment of any *sensible Good*, that without it, neither *Riches*, nor *Honours*, nor any thing that we esteem most gratifying to our Senses will signifie any thing at all to us. Now that a *Sound* and *Healthful Constitution* doth exceedingly much
depend

depend upon a difcreet government and moderation of our Appetites and Paffions, upon a
fober and temperate ufe of all Gods Creatures,
which is an *effential* Part of *True Religion*, is a
thing fo evident, that I need make no words
about it. What are moft of our *Difeafes* and
Infirmities that make us miferable and unpittied
while we live, and cut us off in the midft of our
days, and tranfmit Weaknefs and Rottennefs to
our *Pofterity*, but the effects of our *Exceffes* and
Debauches, our *Wantonnefs* and *Luxury*? Certainly, if we would obferve thofe Meafures in our
Diet and in our *Labours*, in our *Paffions* and in
our *Pleafures* which Religion has bound us up to,
we might to fuch a degree *Preferve* our *Bodies*, as
to render the greateft Part of *Phyfick* perfectly
fuperfluous. But thefe things are too well
known to need to be infifted on. I therefore
pafs on to the next thing.

Secondly, *A Life of Religion doth very much
increafe the relifh and fweetnefs of all our fenfible
Enjoyments.* So far is it from abridging us of
any of our earthly delights (as its enemies flan-
deroufly reprefent it) that it abundantly height-
ens them. It doth not only indulge to us the
free Ufe of all thofe good Creatures of God
which he hath made for the Support and Com-
fort

fort of Mankind, while they are in thefe Earthly Bodies; but alfo makes them more exqui-
fitely gratifying and delightful than without it
they could poffibly be. And this it doth in part
by the means of that never fufficiently commended Temperance and Moderation I before
fpoke of : for hereby it comes to pafs that our
Senfes, which are the Inftruments of our Pleafures are always preferved in that due Purity
and Quicknefs, that is abfolutely neceffary for
the right performing of their *Offices*, and the
rendering our Perceptions of any thing grateful and agreeable. Whereas the *Senfual* and
Voluptuous man defeats his own defigns, and
whilft he thinks to enjoy a *greater* fhare
of *Pleafures* than other men, really enjoys a
lefs. For his Diffolutenefs and giving up the
reins to his Appetites only ferves to dull and
ftupifie them. Nor doth he reap any other
Benefit from his continual hankering after *Bodily Pleafures*, but that his *Senfations* of them
are hereby made altogether *Flat* and *Unaffect-
ing*. Neither is his *Meat* half fo favoury, nor
his *Recreations* fo diverting, nor his *Sleep* fo
fweet, nor the *Company* he keeps fo agreeable
as *Theirs* are, that by following the meafures
of

of *Nature* and *Reafon*, come to them with *truer* and more *unforc'd* Appetites.

But befides this, there is a certain *Lightfomnefs* and *Chearfulnefs* of mind, which is in a manner *peculiar* to the truly *Religious* Soul,that above all things *fets off* our *Pleafures*, and makes all the *Actions* and *Perceptions* of Humane Life *Sweet* and *Delightful*. True *Piety* is the beft Cure of *Melancholy* in the world; nothing comparable to it for difpelling that *Lumpifhnefs* and *Inactivity*, that renders the Soul of a Man uncapable of enjoying either it felf or any thing elfe. It fills the Soul with perpetual *Light* and *Vigour*, infufeth a ftrange kind of *Alacrity* and *Gayety* of Humour into us. And this it doth not only by removing thofe things that *Hinder* our Mirth, and make us languifh in the midft of our Feftivities, (fuch as are the Pangs of an Evil *Confcience*, and the ftorms of unmortified *Paffions*, of which I fhall fpeak in the following particular) but even by a more *Phyfical Efficiency*. It hath really a mighty Power to *Correct* and *Exalt* a mans *Natural* Temper. Thofe Ardent Breathings and Workings wherewith the Pious Soul is continually carried out after God and Virtue, are to the Body like fo much *Frefh Air* and *Wholfom Exercife*, they *Fan* the

F   *Blood*,

Blood, and keep it from *Settling*; they *Clarifie*
the *Spirits,* and purge them from thofe groffer
Feculencies which would otherwife *Cloud* our
Underftandings, and make us *dull* and *liftlefs.*
And to thefe effects of *Religion* doth *Solomon*
feem to Allude, when he tells us, that *Wifdom maketh a mans face to fhine,* Ecclef. 8. 1.
· Where he feems to intimate, that that *Purity*
and *Exaltation* into which the *Blood* and *Spirits*
of a man are wrought by the Exercife of Virtue
and Devotion doth diffufe it felf even to his
Outward Vifage, making the *Countenance* clear,
and ferene, and filling the *Eyes* with an unu-
fual kind of Splendor and Vivacity. But whether this be a true Comment on his words or
no, certain it is, that *Piety* difpofeth a man to
Mirth and *Lightnefs* of Heart above all things in
the world : and how admirable a *Relifh* this
doth give to all our other *Pleafures* and *Enjoyments* there is none but can eafily difcern.

Thirdly, Let it be further confidered, that
Godlinefs is a moft Effectual *Antidote* againft all
thofe *Inquietudes*, and *Evil Accidents*, that do either wholly *deftroy*, or very much *embitter* the
Pleafures of this Life.
For whilft it teacheth us to place all our Happinefs

pinefs in *God Almighty* and *our felves* only,
whilft we have learn'd to bring all our Affections and Paffions, our Defires and Averfions,
our Hopes and Fears, under the command of
our *Reafon*, and endeavour not fo much to
fuit *Things* to our *Wills*, as our *Wills* to *Things*;
being Indifferent to all Events that can happen, fave only that we always judge thofe Beft
which God in his Providence fends us. Being
I fay, thus difpofed (as certainly Religion if it
be fuffered to have its perfect work upon us
will thus difpofe us,) what is it that fhall be
able to difturb or interrupt our *Pleafures*, or
create any Trouble or Vexation to us? Our
Prefent Enjoyments will not be *Embittered* with
the fear of lofing them, or *leffened* by our Im-
patient Longing after *Greater*. Our *Brains* will
not be upon the *Rack* for Compaffing things
that are perhaps Impoffible, nor our *Bodies*
under the Scourge of *Rage* and *Anger* for every Difappointment. We fhall not look pale
with *Envy* that our *Neighbours* have that which
we have not, nor Pine away with *Grief* if we
fhould happen to lofe that which we have.

But the *Vicious* man is expofed to all thefe
Miferies, and a thoufand more; He carries
that within him, which will perpetually fret

and

and torment him, for he is a *Slave* to his *Paſ-
ſions*; and the leaſt of them, when it is let looſe
upon him, is the *Worſt* of *Tyrants*. He is like
the *Troubled Sea*, reſtleſs and ever working,
rifled and diſcompoſed with every thing. He
is not capable of being rendred ſo much as *To-
lerably Happy* by the beſt Condition this world
affords : For having ſuch a world of Impetu-
ous *Deſires* and *Appetites* which muſt all be *ſatisfied*, or elſe he is miſerable ; and there being
ſuch an infinite number of *Circumſtances* that muſt
concur to the giving them that *SatisfaCtion* : And
all theſe depending upon *Things without him*,
which are perfectly out of his Power , it cannot be avoided but he will continually find matter to diſquiet him , and render his condition
troubleſome and uneaſie : a thouſand unfore-
ſeen Accidents will ever be croſſing his Deſigns.
Nor will there be wanting ſome little Thing
or other, almoſt hourly to put him out of Humour.

And if this be the Caſe of the *Vicious* man,
in the *Beſt Circumſtances* of this world (where
the Cauſes of Vexation are in a manner un-
diſcernable) in what a miſerable Condition
muſt he needs be , under thoſe more *Real Af-
fliCtionS* unto which Humane Life is obnoxi-
ous,

ous, what is there that shall be able to support his Spirit under the Tedioufnefs of a *Lingering Sickness*, or the Anguifh of an *Acute Pain*? What is become of all his Mirth and Jollity, if there fhould happen a *Turn* in His *Fortune*, if he fhould fall into *Difgrace*, or his Friends forfake him, or the Means of maintaining his Pleafures fail him, and the miferable man become *Poor* and *Defpifed?* Not to mention a great many more Evils, which will make him uncapable of any Confolation, eat into the Heart of his beft Enjoyments, and become *Gall* and *Wormwood* to his choiceft Delicacies.

And has he not now, think you, made *admirable* Provifions for his *Pleafures?* Has he not done himfelf a wonderful Piece of Service, by freeing himfelf from the *Drudgery*, as he calls it, of Virtue and Religion? Alas, *Poor Man!* this is the only Thing that would now have fecured him from all thefe fad *Accidents* and *Difpleafures*. The *Good Man* fits above the *Reach* of *Fortune*, and in fpite of all the Viciffitudes and Uncertainties of this *Lower World*, with which other men are continually Alarm'd, enjoys a Conftant and Undifturbed Peace. Thofe *Evils* that may be *Avoided*, (and really a great many which afflict mortal men, are fuch) he by his

F 3   Pru-

Prudent Conduct and Government of himself
wholly prevents. And those that are *Unavoid-
able*, he takes by such a *Handle*, that they have
no power to do him any *Harm* : For he is indeed possessed of that which the *Alchymists* in
vain seek for : Such a *Sovereign Art* he has, that
he can turn the *Basest Metals* into *Gold*, make
such an use of the *worst Accidents* that can befal
him, that they shall not be accounted his *Mise-
ries*, but his *Enjoyments*. So that however the
varieties of his Condition may occasion a *change*
in his *Pleasures*, yet can they never cause any
Loss or *Destruction* of them.

And this security he enjoys, not as some of
the *Stoicks* of old pretended to do, by an Imagi-
nary *Insensibility*, or by changing the *names* of
Things, calling that no *Evil* which Really is one :
but by an absolute Resignation of himself to the
will of *God*, and an Hearty acquiescing in his
wise Providence. He is certain there is a God
that governs the world, and that nothing happens to him, but by his Order and Appointment.
And he is certain also that this God hath a Real
kindness for him, and would not dispense any
Event unto him, but what is really for his Good
and Advantage. And these thoughts so support
his Spirit, that he not only bears patiently, but
thanks

thanks God for what ever happens to him.
And inftead of Fretting and Complaining that
things fucceed otherwife then he expected , he
Refolves with himfelf that that Condition,what-
ever it be, in which he actually is, is indeed beft
for him ; and that which he himfelf, were he
to be the Carver of his Fortunes, fuppofing him
but truly to underftand his own Concernments,
would chufe for himfelf above all others.

But further, befides this fecurity from *Outward Difturbances* which our virtue obtains for
us, there is another *Evil* which it alfo delivers
us from, with which the wicked man is almoft.
perpetually haunted , and which feldom fuffers
him to enjoy any fincere, unmingled Pleafure.
That which I mean is the *Pangs* of an *Evil Confcience*, the Fears, the Reftlefnefs, the Confufion, the Amazements that arife in his foul from
the fenfe of his Crimes, and the juft Apprehen-
fions of the fhame and vengeance that doth a-
wait them, poffibly in this Life , but moft certainly in the Life to come.

How Happy, how Profperous foever the Sin-
ner be as to his other Affairs, yet thefe Furies he.
fhall be fure to be plagued with : no pompouf-
nefs of Condition , no coftly Entertainments,
no noife of Company will be able to drive them
away.

away. Every man that is wicked cannot but know that he is so, and that very Knowledge is a Principle of perpetual Anguish and Disquietude. Be his Crimes never so secret, yet he cannot be confident they will always continue so : and the very Apprehension of this makes him feel all the Shame and Amazement of a present Discovery. But put the case he hath had the good luck to sin so closely, or in such a nature that he need fear nothing from *Men* ; yet he knows there is an Offended *God* to whom he hath a sad and a fearful Reckoning to make : a God too *Just* to be Bribed, too *Mighty* to be Over-awed, too *Wise* to be Imposed upon. And is not *the man*, think you; under such Reflections as these likely to live a very *Comfortable life* ? Ah, none knows the *Bitterness* of them but himself that feels them. To the Judgment of others he perhaps appears a very happy man, he hath the world at his beck, all things seem to conspire to make him a great *Example* of *Prosperity*, we admire, we applaud his Condition. But ah, we know not how sad a heart he often carries under this fair Out-side : we know not with what sudden Damps his spirit is often struck, even in the heighth of his Revellings. We know not how unquiet, how broken
ken

ken his sleeps are, how oft he starts and looks
pale; when the Wife that lies by his side under-
stands not what the matter is with him.

He doth indeed endeavour all he can to stifle
his Cares, and to stop the mouth of his Conscience. He thinks to *divert* it with *Business*, or
to *flatter* it with little *Sophistries*, or to *drown* it
with *rivers* of *Wine*, or to *calm* it with *soft* and
gentle Airs. And he is indeed sometimes so suc-
cessful in these Arts as for a while to lay it asleep.
But alas this is no lasting peace, the least thing
awakens it, even the sound of a *Passing-Bell*,
or a *clap* of *Thunder*; nay, a Frightful *Dream*,
or a *Melancholy Story* hath the power to do it, and
then the poor man returns to his Torment.

And now judge you, whether the Honest and
Virtuous Man that is free from all these Ago-
nies, that is at Peace with *God*, and at Peace with
his own *Conscience*, that apprehends nothing ter-
rible from the *one*, nor feels any thing trouble-
some from the *other*, but is safe from *Himself* and
from all the *world* in his own Innocence : Judge,
I say, whether such a one hath not laid to himself *better* and *surer Foundations* for *Pleasures* and
a happy Life, than the man that by indulging
his *Lusts* and *Vices*, only breeds up a *Snake* in his
Bosom, which will not cease to *Sting* and *Gall*
G   him

him beyond what a Tongue is able to exprefs,
or a *witty Cruelty* to Invent.

Fourthly and laftly, befides the benefits of
Religion for *removing* the *hinderances* of our *Pleafures*; it alfo adds to Humane Life a world of
pleafures of its own, which vicious men are utterly unacquainted with.

..And thefe are of fo excellent a kind, fo delicious, fo enravifhing, that the higheft gratifica-
tions of fenfe are not comparable to them. Never till we come to be heartily Religious do we
underftand what *true Pleafure* is. That which
arifeth from the grateful motions that are made
in our outward fenfes, is but a *faint fhadow*, a
meer dream of it. Then do we begin to enjoy
true Pleafures indeed when our Higheft and Divi-
neft Faculties, which were wholly laid afleep
while we lived the life of fenfe, begin to be awa-
kened, and to exercife themfelves upon their
proper objects, when we become acquainted
with God, and the Infinite Abyfs of *Good* that is
in him, when our hearts are made fenfible of
the great Love and goodwill he bears us; and
in that fenfe are powerfully carried out in Joy,
and Love, and defire after him : when we feel
the *Divine Nature* daily more and more difplayed.
in.

in our fouls, fhewing forth it felf in the bleffed
Fruits of Charity and Peaceablenefs, and Meek-
nefs, and Humility, and Purity, and Devotion,
and all the other Graces of the Holy Spirit. It is
not poffible but that fuch a Life as this muft
needs be a Fountain of inexpreffible joy to him
that leads it, and fill the Soul with tranfcendent-
ly greater content than any thing upon earth can
poffibly do : for this is the Life of God, this is
the Life of the Bleffed Angels above, this is the
Life that is moft of all agreeable to our own natures. While we live thus, things are with us as
they fhould be; our Souls are in their natural
Pofture, in that ftate they were framed and de-
figned to live in : whereas the Life of Sin is a
ftate of Diforder and Confufion ; a perpetual
violence and force upon our Natures. While we
live thus, we enjoy the *Pleafures* of *men*, whereas
before when we were governed by fenfe, we
could pretend to no other fatisfactions but what
the *Brutes* have as well as we. In this ftate of life
we gratifie our *Higheft* and *Nobleft* Powers, the
intellectual Appetites of our Souls; which as
they are infinitely capacious, fo have they an infinite good to fill them : whereas in the fenfual
Life, the *meaneft*, the *dulleft*, and the *moft contra-
cted* Faculties of our Souls were only provided
for.   G 2   But

But what need I carry you out into thefe *Speculations*, when your own *fenfe* and *experience* will afcertain you in this matter above a thoufand Arguments. Do but ferioufly fet your felves to *ferve God*, if you have yet never done it, do but once try what it is to live up to the Precepts of *Reafon*, and *Virtue*, and *Religion*; and I dare confidently pronounce that you will in *one month* find more *Joy*, more *Peace*, more *Content*, to arife in your fpirits, from the fenfe that you have refifted the Temptations of Evil, and done what was your duty to do, than in *many years* fpent in Vanity and a Licentious courfe of living. I doubt not in the leaft, but that after you have once *feen* and *tafted how gracious the Lord is* , how good all his ways are , but you will proclaim to all the world, that *One day fpent in his Courts is better than a thoufand*: Nay , you will be ready to cry out with the *Roman Orator* (if it be lawful to quote the Teftimony of a *Heathen*, after that of the *Divine* Pfalmift) that *One day lived according to the Precepts of Virtue is to be preferred before an Immortality of Sin.*

You will then alter all your fentiments of things, and wonder that you fhould have been fo ftrangely abufed by falfe reprefentations of Virtue and Vice. You will then fee that Religion is
quite

quite another thing than it appeared to you before you became acquainted with it. Inftead of
that grim, fowr, unpleafant Countenance in
which you heretofore painted her to your felf,
you will then difcover nothing in her but what
is infinitely Lovely and Charming. Thofe very
Actions of Religion which you now cannot
think upon with Patience, they feem fo harfh
and unpleafant, you will then find to be accom-
panied with a wonderful Delight. You will not
then complain of the *narrownefs* of the *Bounds*,
or the *fcantinefs* of the *Meafures* that it hath confi-
ned your defires to; for you will then find that
you have hereby gained an entrance into a far
greater and more perfect *Liberty*. How ungen-
tilely, how much againft the *grane* of *Nature* foever it now looks to *forgive* an *Injury*, or an *Af-
front*; you will then find it to be as far more ea-
fie, fo far more fweet than to revenge one. You
will no longer think works of *Charity* burden-
fome or expenfive; or that to do good Offices
to every one is an employment too mean for
you; for you will then experience that there is
no fenfuality like that of *doing good*, and that it
is a greater pleafure to *do* a kindnefs than to *receive* one. How will you chide your felf for having been fo averfe to *Prayer* and other devout

Exer-

Exercises, accounting them as tiresome unsavoury things ; when you begin to feel the delicious Relishes they leave upon your spirit ? You will then confess that no Conversation is half so agreeable as that which we enjoy with God Almighty in Prayer ; no Cordial so reviving as heartily to pour out our souls unto him. And then to be affected with his *Mercies*, to praise and give thanks to him for his Benefits, what is it but a very *Heaven* upon *Earth*, an anticipation of the Joys of Eternity ? Nay, you will not be without your pleasures even in the very *entrance* of *Religion*, then when you exercise acts of *Repentance*, when you *mourn* and *afflict* your self for your sins, which seems the frightfullest thing in all Religion. For such is the nature of that holy sorrow, that you would not for all the world be without it, and you will find far greater Contentment and satisfaction in *grieving* for your *Offences*, then ever you did receive from the *Committing* them.

But, O the ineffable Pleasures that do continually spring up in the heart of a good man, from the sense of Gods Love, and the hope of his Favour, and the fair prospect he hath of the Joy and Happiness of the other world ! How pleasing, how transporting will the thought of these things be to you ! To think that you are one of those
happy

happy fouls that are of an Enemy become the Friend of God, that your ways pleafe him, and that you are not only *Pardoned*, but *Accepted* and *Beloved* by him: to think that you a *poor Creature* who were of your felf nothing, and by your fins had made your felf far worfe than nothing, are yet by the goodnefs of your Saviour become fo *confiderable a Being*, as to be able to give delight to the King of the world, and to *caufe joy in Heaven among the Bleffed Angels by your Repentance*: to think that God charges his Providence with you, takes care of all your Concerns, hears all your Prayers, provides all things needful for you, and that he will in his good time take you up unto himfelf, to live everlaftingly in his Prefence, to be partaker of his Glories, to be ravifhed with his Love, to be acquainted with his Counfels, to know and be known by *Angels*, *Archangels*, and *Seraphims*; to enjoy a Converfation with *Prophets*, *Apoftles*, and *Martyrs*, and all the *Raifed* and *Glorified Spirits* of Brave *Men*; and with all thefe to fpend a happy and a rapturous Eternity, in Adoring, in Loving, in Praifing God for the Infinitenefs of his Wifdom, and the Miracles of his Mercy and Goodnefs to all his Creatures. Can there be any *Pleafure* like this? Can any thing in the world put you into fuch an *Ecftafie* of *Joy* as the
                                                                very

very *thought* of thefe things ? With what a mighty
fcorn and contempt will you in the fenfe of them
look down upon all the little Gauderies and fick-
ly Satisfactions that the men of this world keep
fuch a ftir about!How empty & evanid,how flat
and unfavoury will the beft Pleafures on Earth
appear to you in comparifon of thefe Divine
Contentments ? You will perpetually rejoyce,
you will fing Praifes to your Saviour, you will
blefs the day that ever you became acquainted
with him ; you will confefs him to be the only
mafter of Pleafure in the world, and that you
never knew what it was to be an *Epicure* indeed,
till you became a *Chriftian.*

  Thus have I gone through all thofe Heads
which I at firft propofed to infift on. What now
remains but that I refume the *Apoftles Exhortation*
with which I begun this Difcourfe, that fince as
you have feen, *Godlinefs is fo exceedingly profitable
to all the purpofes of this Life, as well as the other:* fince,
as you have feen, *Length of days is in her right hand,
and in her left hand riches and honour* ; and *all her ways
are ways of pleafantnefs , and all her paths are peace :*
you would all be perfwaded ferioufly to *Apply
your felves* to the *exercife* of it. Which that you
may do, *God of his,* &c.

F I N I S.

www.ingramcontent.com/pod-product-compliance
Lightning Source LLC
Chambersburg PA
CBHW031810090426
42739CB00008B/1239